Liverpool,

Contents

To Roger And Family
Enjoy the Book
Bill. Booth.

Liverpool, Back In The Day

Foreword

This book will focus on some of the special buildings we have lost some of. The 'One Off' Liverpool characters who walked our streets, back in the day.

In every area of Liverpool we have lost dozens of unique buildings. Some institutions that have been lost forever. Our heritage has been stripped bare and not much remains.

Through this book I will place some of them where they originally belonged, the purpose they served, and the holler they left behind, only to be replaced with some form of eye-sore.

We also had in this city dozens of amazing characters. They broke the mould. They simply could not be followed and they were truly original. Today we don't do originality, that's not politically correct. We do Ken and Barbie and everyone follows, just like sheep, all suppressed.

I hope to piece together in pictures, poetry, verse and comments what this great city has and why I think the born and bred Scouser is losing their identity and access to their roots.

Acknowledgements

I would like to thank so many people who gave me the incentive and inclination to write the amount of books which I never thought was possible because I do not know where I found the time.

My thanks goes firstly to Jane who has been a great help in compiling the book in A-Z form.

My friend, Frank Leonard, who has been my driver and gofer while my eye healed after an operation. Chris, the taxi driver, who delivered various material around the charities. Dougie Mannering who supplied countless photographs, not on show while researching the book. My daughters for advertising the books for benefit of the charities we support.

While I am still here I will continue to draw on my knowledge of this great city I love, my youth in Liverpool 5. So, like The Beatles who sang about their city, I write about it and will continue to do so.

Charities to benefit from the sale of W H Booth Jnr's book are:

Zoe's Place Children's Hospice

KIND – investing in children's future

The League of Well-doers who help and serve everyone

A rich heritage in Liverpool.

Chapter 1 – Our heritage demolished

Ann Fowler's House

I have to start with a building close to my heart and a picture of Ann Fowler House, under demolition, a building that served all manner of lovely and destitute people during its life on Netherfield Road. Its founder, Mary Fowler, the mother of Ann, was one of the greatest benefactors to Liverpool and the Salvation Army. Without her there would be no Strawberry Fields Forever, yet never mentioned in the annals of great Liverpudlians. She helped the poor and needy people in her home city. Never to be forgotten was Ann Fowler House. A place to sleep and be in company. Another building that could have been saved. What came in its place, a stretch of grass and the Rupert Dome nearby. But no more Ann Fowler, another building gone from our city.

Schofield's Lemonade

In Dalrymple Street there was literally a stand-out building – Schoies Lemo. Even when it was in the height of production it was a feast to behold. It was without doubt the most popular lemonade in Liverpool. Their wagons were everywhere. It employed hundreds of women and men, every corner shop sold Schofield's lemonade. Yet it closed. How could a name so big just be allowed to fold and die. This is constantly what is being allowed to happen in Liverpool. Even back in the day, but if the business could not survive why should the building suffer? It was truly a unique building that could have been saved and re-used in some form. It could have been made marvellous with a drive-in courtyard. Another piece o Liverpool history gone. In its place is a petrol station. Well that's progress.

The Homer

The Homer was a piece of architecture that could have been saved. It was a beautiful building and could easily have been revamped. The inside stripped of its seats and projection rooms, it need not have been a private property or apartments, but what about a youth club, an indoor sports arena or a snooker and pool facility? Why should a building steeped in heritage like all the great cinemas be lost to demolition? It could have served a purpose to the Liverpool 5 community. Left in its place are commercial units which are a total eye sore. But that's progress.

The Shrewsbury Club

When we were kids, down Greaty there was always plenty of youth clubs to go to. We had the Bronte, the Victoria Settlement, Lee Jones, otherwise known as the League of Welldoers, but the one we preferred as a family was The Shrewsy. That's where my brothers went to. You could play football, darts, snooker. There was a snack bar, it was great. The building as a whole was sound so why did they pull it down? Take a look at it. Did it look dilapidated? No, it was not known what it could have been once done up. I know they built a new club, but I am talking about this building. Ideal student accommodation, deal apartments, then we still would have had the building. More of our heritage taken away. A waste.

Tommy White Gardens

A virtual stronghold, why did it go? There was nothing wrong with the building. It housed hundreds of families, incorporated lifts and you have first time buyers fighting over moving in. Why did it go? Paul McCartney lived there when his mother was a nurse on the district. It does not make sense as a landmark building could so easily have fitted into the Everton scheme of things we still have when renovated the library at the top of Beacon Lane. We still have St Georges Church. We still have The Mere Bank Pub, one of my most liked buildings in the Everton area. We still have the Old Thistle Public House, now under a new name. But land from Everton Park has been reclaimed and now it's not only a thriving pub but a hotel. It proves a point that like the Thistle and the Mere Bank they have people coming into their premises. That's what has been destroyed. They have taken away from the area people. That's why local churches do not get full houses, local pubs rely on football trade. But if you could have saved Tommy Whites then you would have had thousands of people in the area not blades of grass. As pretty as it is, it could have been full of students in Liverpool. Today we have become obsessed with student accommodation. The buildings that now house them are an eye sore. They do not mix well with the old well-built buildings of yesteryear.

If you could image if the city planners had the same vision as the proprietor of JD Wetherspoon chain, he has taken old well-established buildings who are of great benefit to our heritage and created somewhere for people to go in the area. He has created work for thousands of people. Why has the council not done the same for your iconic buildings in Walton, Kensington, Anfield, Everton, etc.

All your great school buildings have gone. Penryn Street, what a building, what a community that could have been with its roof top restaurant etc. St Anthony's School, Schofields Lemonade, amazing architecture. If they had been kept renovated and filled with commerce and people we would have retained at least 50% of the mass of people that left.

If you retained one side of a street and took away your back-to-back neighbours then you renovate and extend your two-up two-down to four-up, a bathroom downstairs extension including kitchen. Do away with the yard, the entry and develop a garden. That way 50% of the area still live there in better up-to-date conditions, coupled with the building retained that would be employing local people, public houses would benefit once renovated to cater for the 50% of people left. That way you keep your buildings and commercial properties. The area would still be there with your schools to educate the area, places to socialise, pubs, cinemas, etc. You would also have been your green space but very few people to use it, it's the cart before the horse situation.

In Liverpool they retain their heritage purely for tourists, municipal buildings, the Bridwell to name two, but remember this is the city not the outskirts where the Scouse heart beat louder. No, we need to retain what we have in areas like Everton, Vauxhall, Dingle, etc. Liverpool people need to fight to keep what planners wish only to be seen in history books. My opinion.

Anderson Street

This picture depicts a normal summer's day in Anderson Street, off Greaty. Take a good look at the few terrace houses. Do they look like slums? If those four houses had a lick of paint, new windows, pointed, etc they would not be out of place in Woolton. But what makes them deemed as unsuitable to live in? We lived in one for 15 years as kids and my parents before me. No, we were part of a slum clearance area whether we liked it or not. The people who lived in them houses kept them spotless. As I have previously said, renovate them and instead of two streets going to be demolished you would only have one. It would have made sense to retain the community.

Rossie School

Take a good look at this picture of Roscommon Street School. Imagine a complete refit and external renovation. You could have a raised terrace area and three floors on either side. That is a minimum of 100 dwellings with three playgrounds and tenant parking. Why was it demolished? It would have fitted in very nicely with Everton Park as it is today. Again we would have kept people in the area if they had kept these buildings of interest and turned them into accommodation. The other 50% of people made to move could have stayed and lived in these buildings in the community for example.

John Bagot Hospital was an ideal apartment location in its own grounds. Ann Fowler's Hostel, Schofields Lemonade, Penryn Street School, The Homer Cinema, all of these buildings of historical interest could have been saved and we would still have had a community. Why not?

Elias Street

They don't look like slums. This street to me as a young boy growing up in the next street to Elias Street, I always thought it was one of the prettiest streets down Greaty. It had a lot going on. There were two wood yards, one coal yard and three general/sweet shops.

My favourite shop was Lizzie Moss's. She was a lovely lady and she kept the shop spotless but me and my brothers would put one shilling a week away in her sweet club for our Easter eggs and Christmas selection boxes. It was saving up and being given the goods twice a year which shaped us into what we are today. Elias Street holds great memories.

Penrhyn Street School (Penny)

Take a look at this building. It was where I started my education. It was blessed with a rooftop playground and it had a cellar gymnasium and dinner hall. It does not take much imagination what this building could have been right in the middle of Greaty.

Well we will start with a terrace restaurant once lifts had been fitted. There were two turrets that could house ten apartments. A further 36 apartments on the front, 36 on the back and 16 either side. That's over 100 dwellings. A commercial business on the top floor and a commercial business in the cellar. Plus a car park for residents. Where it is demolished take a look at it and tell me would that still be here today. Yes without renovation, why not?

John's Chippy in Conny

Situated by the entry in Conway Street, to me it was the best chippy purely because it was literally a stone's throw from where we lived in Gordy. It was very small. You could not fit six people in waiting. It never looked any different. John was very strict and he has kids. He looked hard. He always had his sleeves rolled up with Popeye muscles so you behaved in there. They clearly were not the best around but you could get scallops and they were cheap and that's what counted for my mum.

Chapter 2 – Liverpool Poems

Seth Davy A Liverpool Legend

He sat on the corner of Bevington Bush
Astride of a old packing case
And the dolls on the end of the plank they went dancing
As he crooned with a smile on his face

Come day go day
Wishing my heart for Sunday
Drinking buttermilk all the week
Whiskey on a Sunday

In 1905 old Seth Davy died
And his song was heard no more
And the three dancing dolls
In a Towler bin ended
And the plank went to mend a back door

Come day go day
Wishing me heart for Sunday
Drinking Buttermilk all the week
Whiskey on a Sunday

W H Booth

Comments

This man was a true legend back in the day. When people literally lived on the streets making a living. Be it in pennies, in all weathers. Tucked into his overcoat, his means of a day to day existence in them bleak Victorian days. "Hi Three Dancing Dolls" his means of survival, his endeavour to conquer starvation while bringing amusement in song to all those weary people back in the day in Liverpool.

River Mersey

The river stands majestic surrounded on all sides
By history in its building
By ships that have passed by
Yet you trundle on forever
Amidst the changing sky
The river has been our livelihood
It's graced a thousand years
It has carried souls to far off lands
Amidst their hopes and fears
It's always been a lady too
So gentle in its ways
From King John's words
It's lasted all these days

The river it takes its daily toll
And grades all that's new
It ebbs its way through history
Without a bling or two
It has always been there for us
The passion and the fear
The river it remains sublime
In every passing year

She will always be in our blood
As the waves bombard the quay
But all our wealth
Rest on this soul
That is the River Mersey

W H Booth (Circa 2015)

Comments

The river has always been very dear to me as I ended up being a merchant seaman like my dad, grandad and grandad John Warburton. It's in our blood.

Liverpool 5 – Salt Of The Earth

To be a part of Liverpool 5
You're really very lucky
It is the heart of Liverpool
It vibrates a real warm glow
The people who live and work there
They already know

It has a certain buzz
A place to hang your hat
It has a certain magic
A role not easily found
It echoes through its buildings
To touch the people on the ground

We often think and wonder
Of how it would have been
If Greaty, Scotty and Neddy
Were only just a dream
It places our name in history
Among the real true greats
In Liverpool 5 we are alive
As history dictates

So here's a toast to Liverpool 5
A credit to our name
The meaning of these words
Will never ring the same
Its history is behind us
Its future is looking bleak
It will never be the place it was
When it was at its peak

W H Booth Jnr, Circa 2019

Comments

The place to be when we were kids and free as a bird. A place to play to discover a melting pot of old and new amidst the backdrop of real history in its buildings. A place to hang your hat. That's what Liverpool 5 meant to me and my family, it was home.

The Boothies – She laughed more than she cried

As four we worked together
We formed a real good bond
No-one else could match us
Together we were strong

We were up before the dawn
And out and on the streets
While everyone else was sleeping
The Boothies bagged their treats

They never knew what hit them
We really were that good
We tried to be so crafty
As anybody would

We were only children
Trying to do good
Foraging in the jungle
For rags, metal and wood

We tried to help many people
I think we meant to do good
We came, we took, we delivered
Like your proverbial Robin Hood

W H Booth, Circa 2019

Comments

Right through our childhood we were close. We brought each other up and looked out for one another. We were all different yet we were all the same. Boys and girl we all played our parts on life's journey. Our parents would be proud. Billy, John, Alan, Ray, Wayne, Gail.

The Boothies,

Chapter 3 – Various Liverpool Poems

The Reds are on the Wembley trail
They're heading for the top
There's dancing down on Scotty Road
And singing from the Kop

Up Anfield Way
The world is gay
All Scousers' hearts a tingle
There's bags and bags of crimson flags
From Bootle to the Dingle

The toast is to eleven men
Who wear the scarlet jersey
Their name will live forever more
Along the River Mersey
They take their place in history
Among the real true greats
Hunt, St John, Thompson, and skipper Ronny Yates

So here's a toast to Liverpool
A credit to the game
Let us hope on May the first
The cup will bear your name

So sing out Eey Aye Addio
On Wembley's famous ground
Let London towns re-echo
To your famous Mersey sound

L.F.C. Circa 1964-65

The Miracle of Istanbul

The 96 were watching
As we walked out in Istanbul
Shanks, Bob and Emlyn
Were looking down as well

It seemed to be all over
When Milan scored their three goals
But someone else was watching
And that man was a Pole

So the folks up there in heaven
Were a little bit surprised
When Pope John Paul the Second
Appeared right before their eyes

He smirked at Shanks and Paisley
And Emlyn knelt and said some prayers
They turned back to the lads and said
I have just spoken to him upstairs

He can't do much that obvious
But he will see what he can do
He thinks it might be better
If you played a 3-5-2

He saw the team struggling
And that Finnan needs a rest
But don't worry lads cause now
The keeper's gloves are blessed

You see the lad between the net is one of mine
So I put in a request
I know I lived in Italy down in the Vatican
But I can't quite bring myself
To be shouting for Milan

So the word's gone down to Rafa
To do the best he can
He whispered very quietly
He do better with Hamman

He says you will be alright from now on
The game it is not dead
And things will soon get better
If young Steve uses his head

It was Vladis birthday yesterday
And the man owes him some luck
He'll even do the decent thing
And make Milan Baros duck

We owe Xavi a big favour
Because of his broken leg
But he will need to follow up
And score with his left peg

And then just to make it interesting
He has ordered extra time
And we'll see how good them gloves are
When Dudek saves it off the line

We've done everything we can
To make sure the ball stays out
But we cannot interview a penalty shoot out

So Shanks, Bob and Emlyn
And good old Pope John Paul
Watched the match in wonder
And cheered on every goal

And full time went to extra time
With the fans nervously sick
And they waited until the time came
For Sergino's first spot kick

Sergino missed the goal
And Pirlos shot was saved
But Did and Lord Frodsham
Proved their nerves were not as frayed

Then Thomason put one in
And Risle missed his shot
Then Kaka scored, and Smicer scored
The atmosphere was red hot

Then almost in slow motion
It was time for Shevenchenkos chance
But Dudek had different ideas
And done a little dance

Then waited for a second
As the ball came flying in
Dived to the right and parried it
To save it for the win

And as they looked down on the fans
And scenes of abandon
Em turned to Old John Paul
And put his arms around him
And said that was unbelievable
The best game without a doubt

But I thought you said you would not help
With the shout out
John Paul looked up and smiled and said
Look son it was not me
And I wouldn't doubt the word of God
In truth and honesty

So Emlyn was so puzzled
As the ground was growing wild
But in the corner on the cloud
Shanks and Paisley sat and smiled

The moral of this story is
That money can't buy success
And neither can a constant whinge in the Press
And writing a team off
When the clock reaches half time
A just result in something coming out of the Divine
Because Shankly and Paisley knew the cup was coming home
God wars the red of Liverpool
And you will never walk alone

This poem was written by a true red with Divine intervention.

The Shanks

When Shankly came to Liverpool
And walked towards the Kop
He touched our hearts
He never came in a flash fur coat
Or smoking his big cigar
He came across as one of us
Whose philosophy was simple

And so to what was once the fame
The Kopites had at their feet
All that left is the memory of the man
Whose voice was warm
Would make your heart tingle
But no more will his voice be heard
In the grounds he used to mingle

So come on all you Scousers
Let's hold our heads up high
And think about these glory days
When the Shanks left Scotland
To be an honorary Scouser, och aye

Manager, LFC, YNWA, Circa 1958-1974

Comments

The man who single handed transformed a run-down football club into a bastion of invincibility and with his vision placed Liverpool Football Club as the most successful team in the United Kingdom and the most feared team in Europe. Currently the best team in the World, won in 2019.

Forever the Shanks.

W H Booth Jnr

Liverpool, Back In The Day

In goes your eye out

> You walk outside
> You take your share
> You think it's all worthwhile
> A smile of hope
> A smile of joy
> A smile of grief and sorry
> A life today
> A death tonight
> Who knows who says tomorrow
>
> When this old world
> It get you down
> There's no much left to say
> Just drink your drink
> And eat your jam
> And die from day to day
>
> RIP

W H Booth Jnr

Comments

The moral of this poem is that you can never take anything for granted. It has a habit of getting your eye wiped when you think it's over it's not. It comes back and bites you on the arse.

Over The Moon

When every day has ended
And a new one just begun
We revel in the joyous light
Of everything we have done

It's ever changing visions
Brings the warmness of each day
And spreads its veins of happiness
Here we go for work and play

Our hopes and fears
Are so intense
As we glimpse for pleasures new
And hope and pray
That each new day
Keeps the sunshine shining through

Our childhood days
And sun filled joy
Means we will always have you
And soon we will be over the moon

W H Booth Jnr

Comments

This poem depicts our hopes and fears when growing up. Will there
be a silver lining? Will I be happy? Will I be rich? Who knows? What will
be will be.

Kids

Inside here is no salvation
From time to time
No way of remaining worthwhile
No hope no salvation
No fear no joy
Just a word called the past
When I was a boy

I envy their faces
All covered in dirt
The way that they laugh
When others get hurt
The food in their stomachs
Some good and some bad
As I cling to the memories
Of when I was a lad

W H Booth Jnr

Comments

This poem I am sure is most children growing up. You explore, you go where only children go with no fear. With dirty faces and dirty hands and that all comes with being a kid.

Content In The Knowledge

It only seems like yesterday
When we were face to face
And memories keep flooding back
At such a pleasing pace
And every day I think of you
I know that this will be
A common part of all my days
That keeps you close to me

As days go by
And weeks turn into years
The memory of your smile
Alleviates the fears
And yet I feel less troubled now
And know that you are safe
'And I as well as you my Harold'
Have that same smile upon my face

W H Booth Jnr

Comments

A real tear-jerker. This is a love lost. A special person gone forever.
Yet the smile lives on in this poem. 'To Harold written for Ivy'. God bless.

In Riverside We Trust

For sixteen years we attended
A unique and special place
We all went there happy
With a smile upon our face

Although we were all different
They taught us all the same
In Riverside we are proud
To glorify your name

The teachers they were varied
They had a real warm glow
We're glad that we three sisters
Played a part in every show

It was not just across the road for us
It would have been a million miles away
But dead on nine, we were in line
For another special day

W H Booth Jnr

Comments

Our youngest daughter, Kate, the youngest of three girls. Herself and Barry also have three girls. Déjà vu! The three granddaughters, Caitlin, Chloe, Evie, attended the same school. In this poem I have captured these young years in a special place surrounded by special people, teachers and students alike. Less we forget our school days.

What Is A Senior Citizen

A senior citizen is one who was here before the Pill
Television, contact lenses, frozen food
Credit cards, and before man walked on the moon
For us time sharing meant togetherness
Not holidays
And a chip meant a piece of wood
Hardware meant nuts and bolts
And software was not even a word

We got married first
Then lived together
And thought cleavage was something butchers did
A stud that fastened a collar to a shirt
And going all the way meant staying on a double decker bus, to the
bus depot

We thought that fast food
Was what you ate in Lent
And a Big Mac was an oversized raincoat
And crumpet we had at tea

In our day grass was mown
A pot was something you cooked in
Coke was something you kept in the shed
And a joint was cooked on Sundays

We are today's senior citizens
A happy bunch when you think how the world has changed
Live you life and learn
Life is but a gold fish bowl
Which some of us choose not to leave
Sad, so sad

How You Know You're Getting Old

Everything hurts
What does not hurt does not work
The gleam in your eye
Is the sun shining on your bifocals
You feel like the morning after
But you have not been anywhere

Your children begin to look middle aged
You join a health club but don't go
A dripping tap starts an uncontrollable urge
You have all the answers
But nobody asks you any questions
You look forward toa a dull evening
You need glasses to find your glasses
You turn out the light for economy
Not romance

You're in a rocking chair
But can't make it go
Your knees buckle but your belt won't
Your back goes out more than you do
Your house is too big
Your medicine box is not big enough
You sing your teeth into a steak and they stay there
Your birthday cake collapses from the weight of all your candles

Stay young as long as you can.

Comments

This poem or verse takes a lifetime to write because you need to have experiences. All above wrote by a very astute pensioner who has a great knack to translate into words her aches and pains.

Stay young as long as you can.

Look Nurse

What do you see nurse, what do you see?
What are you thinking when you look at me?
A crabbie old lady not very wise
Uncertain of habit with faraway eyes
Who dribbles her food and makes no reply
When you say in a loud voice
'I do wish you'd try'

Who seems not to notice
The things that you do
And forever is losing a stocking or shoe
Who unresisting or not
Lets you do as you will
With bathing and feeding your long night to fill

Is that what you're thinking, is that what you see?
Then open your eyes, nurse
You're not looking at me

I'll tell you who I am as I sit here so still
As I move to your bidding
As I eat at your will
I'm a small child of ten
With a father and mother
Brothers and sisters
Who love one another

A young girl of sixteen
With wings on my feet
Dreaming that soon a lover she'll meet
A bride soon at twenty
My heart gives a leap
Remembering the vows I promised to keep

At twenty five now
I have a young of my own
Who needs me to build
A secure happy home
A woman of thirty
My young are growing fast
Bound to each other
With ties that will last

At forty my young now soon will be gone
But my man stands by me
Too see I don't mourn
At fifty once more
Babies play round my knee

Again we know children
My loved one and me

Dark days are upon me
My husband is dead
I look at the future
I shudder with dread
For my young are all busy
Rearing young of their own
I think of the years
And the love I have known

I am an old woman now
And nature is cruel
Tis her jest to make old age
Look like a fool

The boy is grumbling
Grace and vigour depart
Now there is a stone where I once had a heart
But inside this old carcase
A young girl still dwells
And now and again my battered heart swells

I remember the joys
I remember the pain
And I am loving and living my life once again
I think of the years that are so few
All gone so fast
Oh yes they do

So open your eyes nurse
Open and see
Not a crabbie old woman
Look closer, see me

Comments

This poem depicts by a person I never knew but wherever she goes or wherever she roams. I'll treasure these words of woman well told. Her life, her toil her sorry, her pain. These words that she wrote I will try to retain.

This poem should be given to all those not blessed with a soul who think they have a right to de-humanise another human being. Don't judge a book by its cover.

W H Booth Jnr

I Am Fine Thank You

When I was young my slippers were red
I could kick my heels right over my head
When I grew older my slippers were blue
But I could still dance the whole night through
Now as I am old my slippers are black
I walk to the shop and puff my way back

I get up each morning and dust of my wits
Pick up the paper and read the obits
If my name is still missing
I know I'm not dead
So I get a good breakfast
And go back to bed

Another classic. One day at a time, sweet Jesus.

Chapter 4 – Cars back in the day

When I was a boy there were no cars parked in our street. There were a few handcarts. A car I always dreamed I would one day own was the Jaguar. It was the business, even then in the late 50s and early 60s.

At the bottom of Gordon Street there was a scrap yard and the owner was Alfie Packenham. He had a Jag. It was the best around, nothing touched it.

I was in love with it from day one as a boy. To this day it is the only car at the moment we are working, but as soon as I retire that is my first port of all.

I used to admire the car from afar. Each week it came out to be washed and polished by Paki's assistant who gave it a good valet. I said to Paki, short for Packenham, one day when we were getting told off for playing football too close to the Jag. One day I will have one of them.

His reply was very credible. I don't doubt that Booth, he said. I know what you're capable of now go and play somewhere else. Because of the respect I had for the car, Paki was a lucky man. Of course there were dozens of cars that came up to scratch.

Them days my father in law, Walter Deck – Wally drove some lovely cars during his life. He had a Humber Snipe, a Wolsley, a Riley, all big cars. When he retired he bought a new Volkswagon. It was orange but he loved it to the end.

My memory of big cars was when I was working for Addisons Dairies in Bedford Road, Walton. They had a fleet of big cars, Princess, Wolseys. To me as a boy I thought they were loaded. But of course they were not, they were self employed and they worked long hours and deserved to reap the benefits of their labour. They had the best cars around and good luck to them. Myself and my wife Cathy know what it is like to put in long hours to build up a business and be in control of your own destiny. We obviously have not done too much wrong having just celebrated our 51 years in business and still working. And our 50 years married.

Another company I worked for, Sprakes Engineers, off Gt Howard Street, all the sales staff, directors, etc, all had prestige vehicles, Jaguar, Mercedes, Bentleys, etc.

They were well established in their field and had contracts with major factories, building companies and export and their building is still there today.

Chapter 5 – Boys, Birds, Booze

Starting with the boys, in the 1950s and 60s where do I start?

The boys them days were either football stars or pop stars as they were called back in the day. Nobody to be honest of our age then thought about anything else. Of course there were girls, or birds, back in the day.

In the sixties no-one was into political correctness. Then it was not part of the scene. To describe various things, words etc with 50s-60s meanings, groovy swinging people understood what was meant. No malice was intended. Today people are old before they have lived.

We were only teenagers, 13-15, we were into The Beatles, Stones, The Who. They were all at their peak then. It was flower power, the Beach Boys, the Monkees. The whole journey was about youth. We were kids.

The iPad, Blackberry, mobile, Bluetooth etc, all them gadgets stop you enjoying yourself. Facebook, just think you might miss someone having their tea in case they're having something new. Who cares? We got on with our lives not other peoples.

As teenagers we would follow Liverpool, Everton, England, all successful, all never to be repeated.

At that time in the sixties we had Bobby Moore, Gordon Banks, Alan Ball, Roger Hunt, Jimmy Greaves, real men, not like today's players. 'Where's me mam?' Rock on VAR – Vocal Aggressive Robots. Look at me, look what I've got. Barbie and Ken.

We had Ian St John, Tommy Finney, Stanley Matthews. They were stars, real legends, not celebrities.

Bill Shankley, Harry Catterick, Brian Clough, Bill Nicholson, Matt Busy, Jock Stein, real managers who won trophies. Today you can go to your grave without winning a trophy yet have millions in the bank by helping a club not get relegated. I can do that. What a CV. Most of the above even got a bus home.

Players and managers back in the day even cleared snow. Come on, today's players are wearing gloves in May. Managers and players stayed loyal to their clubs for years. Money was poor but they were loyal. Today players stay two years, walk away with millions, next stop Benidorm. Back then team shad no more than 15 players, today they have 40.

We had Ali, Liston, Patterson, Joe Louie, all hard men, fighting for one belt not ten. There's that many belts today you and even be undisputed champion of Aldi. Sorry, no credibility.

We had dart players like Jocky Wilson, Eric Bristow, John Lowe, etc. Real men who could drink a pint or two. Today they're on petal water. Look out I am mean.

Snooker players all one offs. Alex Hurricane Higgins, a legend, who even had the cheek to try and drink Oliver Reed under the table. Come on, you never knew what you were going to get. George Best, all the so-called rebels. They had to be better than what we have today. 'Don't say this', 'don't say that', 'you can't do this', 'you can't do that'. Tell me what generation engaged themselves. It is obvious, 50s, 60s, 70s, after that we all done as we were told. So sad.

Today we have a dedicated follower of copying as the Kinks once sang. When we went out for a night out with the lads we would kick off, them days, with a pint of Double Diamond, then it was a new drink. No lager, what is that? No, you either had a brown mixed or a black and tan or a Double Diamond. We never drank wine, vodka or JD. What's that?

I had to be different. I only drank bottled Guinness. Come on, that's a drink. Try six of them. At 16-18 years old no need for speed or energy drinks, what are they? If you had a few bob and went into a Bents Pub you could have a glass of Bass and a Bentox. If you had more than two or three Bentox, at 16-18 years old you would soon lose track of where the door was. But who cared? Until you got home and then 'Ah ey Mam, what was that for?' 'Get to bed!' 'But I'm seventeen!' 'I know and I'm forty'. Get up and sleep it off and join your dad. Happy days.

We would often after our pub crawl finish off in the Pacific on Walton Road. We then even bevvied, try to get into Blair Hall. Most of the girls in the area would go there. We knew the bouncers so we always got in.

In between going to sea and coming home on leave, I always had money. I was seeing two girls then. Nothing serious, just casual. So I had to watch who I was chatting up as nine times out of ten I was pissed.

I never got in any trouble, there was a lot of hard lads. Ian and Franny and so on, but with four other brothers I was well protected even though I was the eldest I was never a conformist. I always done my own thing. I don't do sheep. I am still the same today, doing what other people do is for Ken and Barbies. Always forever a rebel to the end.

Chapter 6 – Liverpool pubs

Peter Kavanaghs

We will start around Toxteth and South Liverpool. The first pub has to be the Liverpool 8 jewel in the crown. Peter Kavanaghs situated in Egerton Street. It is a virtual back in the day pub. It is full of nick-nacks, artifacts and memories of a bygone age. The pub itself is spotless. A real diamond, tucked away at the bottom of Egerton Street. It has retained its old-world character yet is surrounded by young and older people of all backgrounds mixing together as if they were all part of a big family. The staff are friendly. It has to be on everyone's bucket list.

Herculaneum Hotel

Known locally as Peglegs, again another pearl of a pub in South Liverpool. Again run by a very experienced lady and it was a popular pub in the area. It has a real tale to tell, it is tucked away but once you find it back in the day, it used to serve the dockers and seamen alike. At the top of the steps just up the Brew and there she stands majestic. It is also a hotel as named the Herculaneum Hotel. Their customers come from near and far. Our cousins from across the Irish Sea and beyond. It has kept its old-world charm while embracing the modern world with all it has to offer and yes, may it be here for a long time, keeping the heritage of pubs close to the river that were written in Liverpool folklore.

The Bramley Moore

While staying close to the waterfront, this pub has a great heritage. It was back in the day a real dockers pub. I myself would call in there when I was on the Empress boats and while with Elder Dempster, my dad was a docker and often worked that end of the Dock Road while I worked at Sprakes, Bibbys and Lamb and Watt. I would make my way there and it was heaving and had great entertainment too. The Bramley had dozens of characters, all steeped in its family atmosphere.

The Cross Keys

Staying in the town, there is not many with a rich history this pub has. While working at Lamb & Watt Shipping Bond in Old Hall Street this was my local. It was well kept. You got good food, bar snacks, entertainment. It was chocker when the stadium was open and all top acts played there. You can keep all your pop-up pubs and your large pubs like Wetherspoons, they may be cheaper but no character. Where the wall and floors, toilets all steeped in Liverpool history and all full of life.

The Mere Bank off Mere Lane in Everton

This pub is a landmark facing Everton Church. It has been there forever. Not as busy as it was back in the day but it puffs along with the help of the football supporters that call in during the season.

It is full of charm, the staff are great and it has retained its character in its various nick-nacks and rooms and has always been a beacon of calm for the older customer. The décor is unreal and it is a pub I use quite often as I prefer pubs with character rather than just spaces. Let it carry on forever.

The Argyles

This pub has seen it all where it sits overlooking Anfield, Stanley Park. This pub keeps reinventing itself and it's always busy. They come from everywhere. It's on the main road in view of Anfield. The clientele is cosmopolitan. It draws people in a pub with charm, class, soul and heart. A real diamond in Anfield.

The Thistle

This pub has had a second chance but it shows you what can be done with reclaimed land. This pub was always popular sitting next to the Everton cinema with the pawnbrokers facing and the competition was awesome on the road with the Campfield, sadly lost forever, with a great history. We had LuLus and of course still have the Mere Bank, another of my ten best pubs but is there on merit as it has been totally revamped, well set out pub, lots of private areas, well decorated, well-kept and a small beer garden and a hotel to boot. Still alive in Liverpool 5.

Ye Hole In The Wall, 4 Hackins Hey

This pub has the lot. History, a place where the good and the great have drank. It's as old as the hills yet still retains that Victorian air of mystique. When you go in you feel someone next to you, someone from the past. We have to retain this pub. It's up there with all that is great about Liverpool. Back in the day it was one of our jewels in the crown. We need to embrace our heritage as this pub as one of the first in Liverpool.

The Willowbank

This pub in Smithdown Road is truly one of Liverpool's greatest. Over the years it has reinvented itself over and over yet it has that pull, mixed clientele, a lovely easy pub to settle in. Full of working class people, academics, students, a real mixed bag. But it keeps going on while all around have gone. The hospital included, which again could have been used to some great purpose but we do have another Asda. Liverpool's future.

The Pig & Whistle

A stone's throw from St Nicholas Church lies this little pub, hidden away. But a pub with some history. It has had somewhat of a chequered past but goes down as one of Liverpool's stopping off pubs for thousands of seamen who will have sailed from the landing stage with either Canadian Pacific, Cunard, Elder Dempster, etc. This pub is mall but very inviting. A couple from down south were there last I went in. The landlord himself entertains tourists. It is a must go pub when you're down that part of the town. You can visit four of the ten I have mentioned within ten to fifteen minutes apart. Surprise yourself next time you're in town.

Remember, these ten pubs are not what the tourist frequent as much purely because they don't have the advertising punch like your supposed pubs in Liverpool. A pub is not about heaving customers, can't hear yourself speak. The traditional pub caters for all customers with places to talk and socialise, check them out. The ten pubs mentioned are not in any order of merit, just what I think as a born and bred Scouser. You may beg to differ. Please do contact me on the office number 0151 427 4161.

Chapter 7 – Liverpool characters

Sandy Brownlow

Let's start with a man who would be down the Pier Head every day, Sandy Brownlow. He would try to keep the kids in order by running after them. He was just trying to keep the peace. A very vocal man he had a disability. He had a club foot which restricted him from moving far but every day he would be on the 26 bus and spent the day in and out of the café, talking to people getting on and off the ferry. Basically, just filling his day. He was a back in the day Scouse character who was well known in Liverpool and mostly down the Pier Head.

John Titchen, The Bird Man

John was a local lad to where I was born. We went to the same school, Rossi. John kept pigeons, as did a lot of lads those days. Down Greaty John was very well known, very clean and popular. He had a loft full of birds. I would often see John in Liverpool town centre at weekends back in the day. He was a character and normally when we had done the pubs we would finish off in the She Club and then onto the Nite Owl Club. He had a great social life in the 70s and 80s and we were all known, including John, around Liverpool.

John Titchen, Buckingham Street

Charlie McCann

This man was a genius with a football. You could not get it off him. He would go around you in circles. He again went to Rossie school. He came from the top of Arkwright Street and in that area there was some great football players back in the day. To name a few, we had Billy Graham, Billy Lambert, Ray Lunt, Alan Young, Terry Ralston, Brian Gaskell. All very talented players, goalkeepers, etc. But around that area, I have to say Charlie was up there on a Sunday afternoon we kids from Gordy would arrange a match with one of the street teams. We were around 12-13. During the game the pubs would let out at two o'clock and the big lads would invade the pitch. They had either been in the Stingo, Orange Club, anywhere around there was pubs everywhere. But once they got the ball Charlie mostly, you would not get it off them. Charlie had still and could mesmerise you with the ball.

Charlie McCann, The Wizard of Greaty, Circa 1950-1960s

Hughie Smith

This man was without doubt one of Liverpool's greatest characters. He never had a lazy bone in his body. I was only young when Hughie was at his peak. But this man was more an entrepreneur than most. When not working he would do all manner of things to enable himself to get a few pints.

Of course, Hughie always skirted around the law but he loved it. It was all about the kill, the thrill of avoidance, and also the booty at the end of the show. And I mean show. He had a great arsenal of tricks up his sleeve and the people of Liverpool loved him.

I mean he was a character not seen today. He physically would gamble with his life for a few bob, most of his escapades were played out around the town centre or down the Pier Head where he and his mate would have a captive audience.

His party trick was to have himself tied up in chains with a lock on it. Bars put through the cloak, he was trust up in, and his job was to do a Houdini act by escaping. He managed it more times than not. On several occasions his mate had done a bunk and Hughie would still be trying to escape while the Police were there. Needless to say he would be very upset that he and his mate had not gone around everybody in the cinema queue who would be eagerly awaiting his return from the sack to applause and then put their coppers in his hat. This would happen most nights in the week or on a Sunday down the Pier Head.

Where his other trick was to lay on the ground with a flag stone, paving stone, on his chest where his mate would steadfastly smash the flag stone with the sledge hammer. Wow! Just for a few coppers for a pint. It would not happen today. Health and Safety would go mad.

Hughie Smith, a Liverpool legend.

Kevin Starkey

This man was a very funny person. I worked with him on the building for years. He was born and brought up down Greaty in Newsham Place and his dad Rob worked with my dad on the barra. He also worked part time in the butchers on Greaty and one of Rod's other sons. Rod worked in Daglish's pawn shop at the bottom of Ellison Street. Kevin just looked funny. He had that manner back in the early 70s he started to come out with a reply each time I would tell him about a bet I had. Just got up when I went into work as it was persistent every other day he started to get fed up with me winding him up and he then started to coin this phrase "Tell me about it". Yes, Kevin Starkey from Great Homer Street first said those words and the world copied. Get on that one.

He worked in Martins Bank off Water Street for four weeks stripping out once it had closed. It was a gold mine. It was full of brass, copper, lead, pictures, amazing wood, door handles, finger plates. We stripped it bare. Some went in the boss's van and the rest, well, two thirds of it went in my mini van. It was me and Kevin's best four weeks in years. We cleaned up. We had a skip outside. While filling the skip the metal would go in the skip, covered with material, then taken out of when finishing work. The mini van was under pressure from the haul each night. How the boss never noticed I don't know. The tyres were practically flat.

One day while filling the skip there was a man close by. We thought he had been collared or it was a time and motion person. It was not. It was a famous Liverpool comedian writing down all Kevin's unique sayings and his quick Liverpool humour. The comedian was John Hackett. Back in the day, Kevin Starkey was original as they come. (No Ken and no sheep.)

John William Walker

This man I had the pleasure and misfortune to have knocked around with and drank with and supported Liverpool with. He was without doubt the man everyone knew, Johnny Walker.

He would run on the pitch every home game in the late 60s and the 70s. He would, if he ever got caught by the Police, take his coat off, put it on the penalty spot and try and score, then he would be escorted out. Only to climb over the wall and be back in the Kop within ten minutes.

Wherever he went,, they knew he would go in a pub or club, stand in the corner and eat a pint glass, right down to the rim, then eat a pound of cheese with crackers. Try that. It's impossible. Johnny would clean up and he never bought a pint.

One day we were in the Thistle in Everton Road. I had just ordered a pint of bitter for Johnny and a bottle of Guinness for myself. Before I could pay the barmaid, Johnny had legged it and I turned round. These two fellas had me up against the bar. 'What's your mate's name?' I could not move, he had just pinched the tin off the bar and ran. I said not guilty mate, I said what was in it, tobacco? 'Don't be funny' he said. It was a time capsule we have just exhumed from the church next door they were demolishing, Everton Church.

While I was ordering the ale, Johnny had heard them say what it was. That's how quick he was. He was fast you could not have caught him he was fast. While trying to plan my case I managed to wriggle free and leg it. I was only twenty five and could run. I never seen him for three days. He must have sold the lot and went on a bender in Birkenhead. When I eventually saw him he made up a story of he dropped it, I know, he was cute.

Another day we were going to watch Liverpool play Man City. I called at Johnny's in St Domingo Grove. When we were going I asked Johnny's wife, Jean, could she wash my car and I would get her some sweets. She only had the brain of a child, she said yes!

Off we went after a few pints we headed for the match. There was thousands of Man city supporters lining Venice Street. We could not pass them. Not Johnny, though, he ran at them calling them all kinds. The Policemen on horseback was nudging Johnny, Johnny ran down one of the entries but it was blocked off. He tried to escape kicking the horse in the ollies. He wriggled out of his coat and ran. Later on in the ground with no shoes on, he asked me for money. I said where's yours? He said the Police have got my coat with m wages in from John West Salmon. Obviously I thought he was lying. He was not. When we got to Johnny's house Jean was on one. Where's me wages, she said to Johnny. You lost them you liar.

Honest, Jean, so then we went to the pub. When we came back all hell let loose. Jean had been down to Anfield Road to get his coat back, check if the wages were in his pocket, which they were. Johnny was arrested. His wages were eighteen pounds. He was up in court on Monday and fined £25. Jean's feet never touched the ground. Her sweet ration was cut down while he had gone to the pub. Jean had washed my mini for pocket money. It was blue when and we came back it was white. She had used a full bottle of strong bleach. It's a classic. Back in the day.

Jagger, Echo Echo

Jagger was our local paperman. Every night, winter and summer, he would shout 'Echo! Echo!'. You could hear him down Greaty. He was well known. He lived in Mona Terrace facing Chapel Gardens. It was a small court like terrace, very old and in need of demolition. He had a wife and son and I can still see him now. Nose dripping in the winter, but he never let you down. Same times he would come with his boy. A real character down Greaty. Also in this picture is the butchers, bottom left, which was run by two women unheard of today. Back in the day.

Chapter 8 – Questions and answers

1. Which Lord Mayor had a sweet shop at the top of Taylor Street?

2. How many scrap yards did the Packenham Brothers own?

3. Where were they situated?

4. What was the first name of the owner of the wallpaper shop facing Sturlas on Greaty?

5. Name Paddy Donnelly's celebrated daughter.

6. Name the bookies facing the Homer.

7. Name one of the pubs, top of Athol Street.

8. Name the company garage top of Dalrymple Street.

9. Name the lady's first name who owned the deli shop facing the cobblers, bottom of Gordon Street.

10. What was the nickname of the wonderful concrete pitch we played on off Neddy Road?

11. Name the three steepest streets off Neddy Road, in your opinion.

12. What street was the Two Gregson Wells pubs top of?

13. Name the street the best street footballer lived in, in your opinion.

14. What street was Daglish pawn shop off Greaty?

15. Who were the Braddocks high rise named after?

16. What street could you buy the best toffee apples off Neddy?

17. Name the headmaster of Penrhyn Street school in 1958.

18. Name the headmaster of Roscommon Street school in 1960.

19. The dance hall above the Co-op in Walton Road, 1950 plus

20. Name the casino/club in Spellow Lane 1960 plus.

21. Name the shop facing the Swan public house at the bottom of Conway Street.

To be answered in Book Five "The Last of the Vindi Boys".

Answers to Questions in Book 3 – The Boothies

1.   Mona Terrace

2.   Jagger

3.   Butchers

4.   Corner Mona Terrace

5.   Johns

6.   Savas

7.   Frankie Hart

8.   Jimmy Melia

9.   Morning Star

10.   Monaghans

11.   Wyndham

12.   The Jester

13.   Chappel Gardens

14.   Stevensons

15.   Aughtersons

16.   Gordons

17.   Melias

18.   ?

19.   Between Gordons and the chemist

20.   Badger

Chapter 9 – Liverpool lost

Bimbo, street cleaner around the Everton Brow area. This man was relentless. You can see from the photo that work was no problem to him in sweltering conditions. He adapted to the weather in order to carry on keeping the area spotless. A real back in the day grafter. Bimbo, a true Scouser.

The Honky Tonk

This was not just any pub, this was one of the best pubs on Scotty. As you can see it was an all singing, all smoking, all drinking real pub with mostly men, so it could have been a Saturday afternoon. Mostly dockers I think, not a white wine or gin to be seen. A real pub back in the day. The Honky Tonk.

Notice no-one seems to be bothered where the smoke ends up or how much they're drinking. It's called life. Before Health & Safety.

Paddy's Market

Will the real Paddy's Market stand up please?

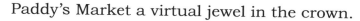

Again, this was no Arndale Centre or swanky market. This is where it all began, generations of down to earth Scousers would visit here from all over Liverpool. Back in the day when money was little and people had to buy cast offs, second hand clothes to clothe themselves and their children, and I for sure was one of them. In the daylight it looked like any other market but in the dark winter days it was dismal. It smelled and rats were everywhere. Yet needs must and Paddy's Market was as popular in South Liverpool as it was on Scotty, Greaty, etc. Even in India where a lot of the seamen who visited Liverpool back in the day would spend their money on hats, coats, suits, shoes, etc.

Paddy's Market a virtual jewel in the crown.

Brunswick Road

With both Gregsons Wells visible it was a busy junction with West Derby Road, with only one policeman controlling traffic. It must have been relentless yet with two of Liverpool's majestic pubs visible the area was exciting and full of shops of all types. Both Gregsons Wells pubs could be full permanently. There was entertainment at the pubs and you also had the cinema the Hippodrome, known locally as the Hippy.

Brunswick Road a hive of activity.

West Derby Road

Looking at this picture from another angle we have just passed the Gregsons Wells Pubs and can now closely see the Hippodrome cinema with Sailor Jacks next door, the famous Liverpool tattooist were all seamen went. We also have Clarkes Gardens, the Liverpool Registry Office, the famous Grafton dance hall and indeed plenty of pubs, Olympic etc.

The Hippy etc West Derby Road, all back in the day.

Heyworth Street

This photo shows how lively a road this part of Liverpool had to offer. Looking at it from the top of Mere Lane it was a road that had the lot. There was a library, the Cast Iron Church, the famous Mere Bank pub. There was chemists, butchers, cake shops, pie shops. There was a haulage company, a cinema even a pawn shop. It had the lot. Sadly gone we still have a school. There is even a couple of pubs that stood the test of time, the Old Thistle, renamed.

The church still stands, thank God. The famous Mere Bank pub is invincible. But the rest sadly is new housing developments and grass. Tons of grass on England's green and pleasant land. Heyworth Street, circa 1967, back in the day.

The Weighing Machine

This photo goes way back in the day depicting Egerton Road. As you can see there was a lot of really fine three-story houses and ample business premises. It's also heavily laden with handcarts and even horse drawn vehicles. The tram lines are very apparent with balustrade around the windows and the old gas lamps back in the day.

Everton Road.

The School Yard

A typical school yard scene during the afternoon break. Notice all the kids, mostly boys, are all wearing short trousers. These traditions have more or less died out now. But back in the day the typical attire for boys at school aged five to eleven was short trousers. We were a real hardy lot.

School yard back in the day.

Scott's Bread

Scott's Bread in Rose Place was a very famous bread maker. The baker vans could be seen all over Liverpool delivering to shops and factories alike. I know that when my brother John was a boy, his first job when leaving school was at this very bakery in Rose Place. He would be up at 4.30am and would start at 5-5.30am, then he would be finished by 11-11.30am for the day. Real hard work but by all accounts, the name Scott's jut went off the radar another big name dies in Liverpool back in the day.

Scott's Bakery

Reece's Down Greaty

Reece's was a big name in Liverpool. There were shops and cafes everywhere. This shop is situated between Mona Terrace and Robsart Street. Notice the Wine Stores. This is around 1955. Com on an offy then. You know there was also facing Reece's cake and cold meats shop was Reece's Dairies on the corner of Chappell Gardens. And just by Stevensons Chippy there was another Wine Store. What a bonus. But it was always said there was no other shopping area like Great Homer Street back in the day.

Conway Street

These houses look uniformed with St Anthony's Church steeples just visible and Sturlas warehouse building standing majestic. You could be anywhere the streets were spotless. The steps were scrubbed bare. And yet they went in the 1960s Council Demolition Act.

Conway Street, back in the day.

Seacombe Street

This was a great street. Look how steep they were and the boys playing football, the Walker brothers, no not the singers. I knew all the boys growing up. Reggie and Johnny were mates of mine. And Jimmy also, their mother and my uncle Jimmy were brother and sister. She was a lovely woman and my uncle was a real gent. Secombe Street also house another uncle of mine, Tommy Meacock, and at the bottom was probably one of the greatest chippies in the world. You would die for the fish cakes.

Seacombe Street, back in the day.

Everton 1970s

Notice the amount of baron land. We called them hollers. I means when a building has been bombed or in this case demolished on a wholesale basis, then all that's left is a hole or space or holler. Just look at the devastation in this photo. All that's left of those iconic streets that once adorned such a rich vibrant community. As you can see the skyscraper there's even a cinema still standing. John Bagot Hospital is still apparent. A school or two still visible before they all will meet their fate. I can still see the remains of what is left of Gordy my old street.

Burrough Gardens Baths and Burlington Street Wash House

In these two pictures you can see how dismal and in need of repair. But the two buildings were the very hub of day to day life in this area off Scotland Road and Vauxhall, in many ways it was. In fact the only social life they had some would visit the wash house two or three times a week, meet up with neighbours and friends, have a good laugh. The same thing applied in the baths. There was always the shower areas and of course the bathing pool for the children. They were very much needed in them days.

Torbo's Barbers

Every shop left boarded up, these shops are off Scotty, top of Hopwood Street. My mate and one of the people who stayed loyal to Scotty Road and is still trading is Tommy Torbo. He has been there 40 odd years. A great barber, we go back years. Tommy has seen the lot on Scotty. When all the pubs were booming I always call in and see him. There are only him and the news shop next door and that side still open, back in the day.

Wilbraham House, off Scotty

This block of flats on Scotty could easily have been retained, revamped, re-modernised and brought up to the present day. At the rear there was balconies, a car park, overlooking Penni school. It would have made near to town centre apartments, near to town centre student accommodation. Next door to the Eagle and alongside the Wilbraham pubs. Why were they demolished so we could have a petrol station in its place? Progress back in the day.

The Piggeries

This is one of a set of high rise accommodation that should never have lasted as long as they did. But eventually after public outcry and media coverage they eventually bit the dust.

The Piggeries of William Henry Street

The Stingo

My spiritual home. It stood at the top of Robsart Street alongside St Polycarps Church. It was always busy for a small pub but when I was working at John Bagot Hospital I would spend a great deal of time there during lunch breaks etc. it was run by Bill and his mum. A great little pub back in the day – The Stingo.

Mazzini and Garibaldi Heights

Not far from Rossi they eventually came to an end. There is now a few houses there but mainly grass.

St Martins Cottages, off Vauxhall Road

We had what was called cottages, but not as we know them. The dwellings were Saint Martins Cottages. Lots of space for the kids to play with St Anthony's Church and Saint Georges in the background. The churches remain, the rest has gone.

Byrom Street

This end of the road had some great pieces of Liverpool heritage. The shop under the flats at Byrom Street end not far from this spot into the wall was a metal tap where you could quench your thirst. More famously there was a fountain built in memory of a famous pub landlord, Dandy Byrne, who managed the Morning Star for years and was an integral part of Liverpool Irish relations in Liverpool at the time. Also a great benefactor to the poor. You notice you never hear of these people when someone in high office or the media are mentioning people who do great things or great Merseysiders. I wonder why? Probably not fashionable enough. Back in the day.

Connie and Robsy

A more later photo of what came after the demolition of Greaty. Here we have two streets so steeped in Liverpool Five culture. In the shadows of the high rise, now part of the mini New York, they don't have the same character as Old Conway Street with John's chippy, Moorcrofts sweet shop, Chris general store and Bill's cellar shop and of course not forgetting St Polycarps Church. Top of Connie the Stingo, top of Robsy the sweet shop, Jack Browns, the Long Room and of course Knoxy Pigeon Loft. A jewel in the crown back in the day.

Off Netherfield Road

Here is an photo of Netherfield Road as we know it today. It looks more like Wally Hall Park. More grass than we expected. Grass is fine if there are playing areas on it. Notice no area for children to play, no goal posts to talk of, no children running around. Just barren. It's all about space, green space. But you can have too much that is doing nothing. My opinion when we had streets you had activity, people interacting. I don't see any of that all. Liverpool back in the day.

Shrewsy and Farmers Arms

Here is a great picture of the bus arriving to take all the kids on a day out or event for an outward bound holiday. The Shrewsy them days were hands on when it came to providing something for the children in the area to go all year round. You can see the maisonettes nearby and you can just see the Farmers Arms pub in Roscommon Street. It was always busy them days. Liverpool back in the day.

This picture depicts the amount of maintenance work that went into keep a busy road looking good. The central reservation separating traffic flowing from north Liverpool to town and town to all areas of Liverpool. The gardeners would plant small shrubs, plants, evergreen, etc to keep it tidy. It would stretch from the end of Great Homer Street up to Virgil Street where there would be approximately three zebra crossings where people would cross. Mostly we would just jump onto the central area and not use the zebra. Liverpool back in the day.

Old Rose Vale

This shot does go way back in the day. It is dark you can just see a hand cart. People talking on the corner of the street. Women talking outside their front doors. It does not paint a great picture of opulence; they were real slums them days. The people had to live in squalor yet remained dignified. Notice the railings outside the windows. Why where they there? To keep people from jumping in their despair. I doubt it purely to decorate the buildings. Liverpool back in the day.

The Midland, Netherfield Rock with Rock View

The bank is sadly not heard of these days yet it stood at the end of Greaty and at the bottom of Everton Valley for years. The building remains.

Inn On The Hill

Sadly this has gone too, the flats too, but the high rise remains. Progress back in the day.

Two greats in name only. One remains and one is part of a tunnel complex. Great Mersey Street had some beautiful Georgian houses. Some still remain. It Was a very majestic street, it could easily have been anywhere in the UK.

Great Nelson Street was steeped in history. It had a great school tucked away. It was the entrance to the great north market which was in my eyes the only market that could bear that name, Greaty Market. Back in the day.

Aughton Street

This is a real winter's day in Aughton Street. It was a very long street, very hilly and as you can see it's starting to look tired. It holds great memories. A couple of lads I knew lived there. Archie Styles and George Walton, school mates of my brothers. Georgie Walton I am not sure but I think Archie went to Venice Street. Don't hold me to that, my opinion. Back in the day.

Daglish Pawn Shop

This building meant so much to the people of the area and it served a great and worthwhile purpose. I would often go in there, a friend of mine Rod Starkey worked there. He told us some stories. He said it was an Aladdin's Cave of goods not picked up. Everything from false teeth to stuffed animals. But it was always busy especially Monday morning. A real part of Great Homer Street history. Ellison Street's claim to fame. Back in the day.

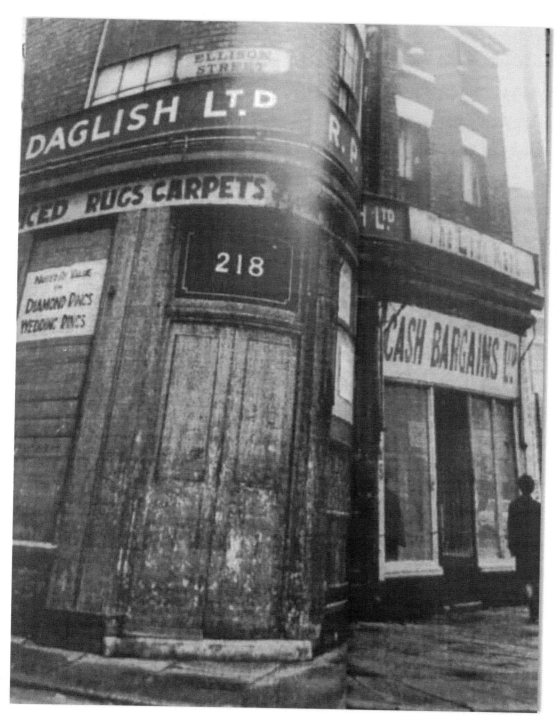

Corrinth Towers

This was a very steep street. It gave you a great view of the high rise mingling with the old streets. How do these cars stay where they are. Notice the shop o the former and the cars. So close to each other. The kids would have a great time coming down this street on their sledge and steering carts.

Back in the day.

William Henry Street, The Piggeries

Notice the three Piggeries at their worst. The shops some closed, the old post box and people unaware of what's around the corner for the Piggeries demolition before all else. A real eye sore. Back in the day.

Two pictures of Cilla outside her old address. Notice Sammy Kam's chippy, Cilla's house or flat above the barbers and the Europa pub, top of Bossi off Scotty Road.

Cilla outside the then boarded up address on Scotty Road in 1978.

The Farmer's Arms Pub

The Farmer's Arms pub in Roscommon Street, a local of mine and my dad's and his mate Tony Bennett in the same street. We had the pleasure of Mr Stanley who found Dr Livingstone I presume ad also the famous cinema and of course our school. What a street.

Again we have Rossi but this time the top and the view of New York New York. Well don't you think so? Not a street in sight. Just high rise and of course more grass. Back in the day.

Genuine stall holder down Greaty back in the day.

Another stall holder down Greaty.   A real hive of activity.

Dorrington Street

Dorrington Street with the church still standing. The inevitable high rise and the now demolished flats and of course the holler.

The high rise top of Rossi, the doctors still standing, the pub still up and landscaping for, you guessed it, high rise. Back in the day.

Off Neddy

Thee flats were facing Robsart Street alongside Mitford Street facing St Polycarps Church. The bus stop as you can see is chocker, waiting for the 46 or the 30 bus. Netherfield Road on any day. Back in the day.

The Tuggy

This pub was a lifesaver. It came after a lot of the pubs had gone and you could go back to Neddy anytime and meet your old mates who would come down regular just to keep in contact with people. It closed and it's an office now. Can you believe that? Back in the day.

Mittford Street

This is one of my favourite photos. It shows life you have St Polycarps Church, you have the high rise. You can see St Anthony's Church and it shows Conway Street and Greaty. Some houses remain. Mittford Street is covered in grass yet the walls we climbed as boys to gain access to John Bagot Hospital remain and still remain to this day. Back in the day.

This picture shows that Coronation Street had nothing on Liverpool 5. Alas all gone as the waste land in the background shows the start of the demolition.

Connie and Gordy

Dreamland Conway Street and Gordon Street, my own street all covered in snow. The holler where we played for the chalice a thousand times looks like a Dickens scene. Back in the day.

Gordon Street and Conway Street

John Bagot, Netherfield Road, Mitford Street, etc, adjacent John Bagot Hospital

Old Rossi

What's left of our old school before demolition. As you can see they have started, the pub, the Windham, will be next, then the school. But the high rise remained a bit longer. Back in the day.

One of the original market women she would have worked with Mrs white on Greaty Market. Be it North Market and St Martins, a true scouse legend. Back in the day.

Braddocks View

This was a typical sight off Neddy. Kids coming down the street at the speed of sound and no brakes and the women going about their business not worrying about them. Why? No Health & Safety, not even a crash helmet. It's called youth. Back in the day.

Rossie

Again Rossie, showing the cinema and the home of Mr Stanley the explorer. It was gracious in its day. Back in the day.

Inside the gym at Rossi school has seen better days. No kids.

York Terrace

These streets stood majestic for all to see. York Terrace in all its glory, a street a terrace that should never have gone. It could be Rodney Street, it could be Bath, it could be the Georgian Quarter, but no, it's Everton and that is getting demolished. Location, location, location, back in the day.

Fairy Street

Another iconic street, Fairy Street. This is where the women that walked up and down here every day never ever needed Iron Bru, or the swill they call today, energy drinks. The men and women who pushed prams up this street were fit. The women, never mind the men, could have played for any football team. They were hard their calfs and legs were bigger than any athlete. The women of Everton never needed any help. They were something else. I defy any person to run down this street or run up it. It was in my eyes the steepest street in Everton. Back in the day.

Great Mersey Street

It could have been anywhere when these houses were built they were awesome and the street oozed class. Some still remain. Back in the day, 1976.

Orange Club

This building is part of the high rise complex in its day. It served as a social club. I know my sister, Gayle, had her reception there. It was on the bend on Need Road. Back in the day.

Robsart Street

All I can say about this photo is kids played out, no indoor kids then. Back in the day.

Typical Kitchen

A typical back kitchen with all the mod cons, damp on the walls, state of the art sink and drainer, modern cooker and a gas lamp on the wall. How did they live back in the day?

The Midland Bank off Neddy

The Midland Bank off Neddy and the Inn On The Hill. The old bank is still standing but the pub has gone. Back in the day.

Chapter 10 – About the charities

This is a picture of my porch at home. For the last thirty years I have decorated my porch with anything that can attract the public. The proceeds from donations each year goes to our chosen charities. This year's these is for 'Keen Gardners Life Outdoors'.

Charities to benefit from donations are:

Zoes Place

K.I.N.D

League of Welldoers

K.I.N.D.

This charity is very close to our heart and we try to help as often as possible.

It is run by a special person who founded the charity in 1975. That's forty five years looking out for and caring and providing for kids in need and distress (KIND). We have visited the premises and seen the good work that is done there and met some of the special people who help out there. And those who donate their time and energy to make sure this special charity goes on for many more years under Steven and David's guidance.

The photo depicts the creative work that goes on in Back Gannon Street and notice the bee hives and gardening and growing pursuits.

Here we have a picture of David. He, along with Stephen, are the driving force behind this remarkable charity.

Mother and daughter. Great help and lovely people. They do a great job and the tea and cake is great.

Another two photos of this wonderful building full of hope and happiness.

Hampers, kitchen goods, etc. Donated each year to K.I.N.D. and Zoes Place Children's Hospice.

Zoe's Place

Zoe's Place is a charity we have supported for over twenty years. We have become so attached to the charity that we fill each year we call with the hampers and gifts that we wish we could do more along with the other charities. We do have all the collection boxes in all our shops in south Liverpool. And my yearly donation to each charity come from the royalties from my books which I wrote to further their coffers, we hope. But I have to say there is no worthy charity than to help small babies live the best of their lives in the care and dedication provided by all staff, from Terry to Carol etc, a great team and a great privilege for me and my family to be associated with.

My mate Frank and Zoe's Place staff member.

League of Welldoers

League of Welldoers have been in this community off Scotland Road in Limekiln Lane, Vauxhall for over 100 years. It is I think the oldest charity in Liverpool. Don't quote me on that however. With Tony and his team what a service they provide for the area and beyond. They do all manner of events, from trips out to Bingo, daily activities, meals on site, picking up pensioners, Tony puts on shows at the Philharmonic Theatre.

It all started way back with Mr L Jones. Lee Jones, to be precise. What a man, what vision, from tiny acorns which this man planted, what a refuge in Vauxhall, in them bleak days when poverty was rife. But there was always Lee Jones as it was then a beacon of hope. Long may Tony and staff provide such a great service.

This picture is my mate's brother, wife and family. He was born in Gordon Street and his wife who worked in Sturlas. He was a seaman like his other two brothers. The three small boys seated are their children. There is a set of twins and the bottom picture depicts the twins today.

Once lost, now found

As we can all see, Liverpool is developing so quickly. If you blink you can miss it. The city of Liverpool now is very much caught up in all things tourism and student care. We have not only become enveloped in those four great boys who really put us on the map, but we now have the sport, the shops, theatres, ferries, Liverpool One, Albert Dock, all our wonderful parks and of course our buildings.

So because of our heritage, our culture the architecture which is second to none which of course is why the film companies use the city so often. In the book as a native of north Liverpool, I have captured a lot of the lost building schools, work places, streets etc from that part of Liverpool.

If these buildings were allowed to drift into history then we have lost the magic they once contained, the memories that were held for those still with us. I feel that all the special buildings in this book have a story to tell, even though most have been lost forever. I hope to continue in this vein in some of my future books which will focus on the great commercial and retail companies Liverpool have had and lost.

W H Booth Jnr

Printed in Poland
by Amazon Fulfillment
Poland Sp. z o.o., Wrocław